HOTTEST COLDEST HIGHEST DEEPEST

STEVE JENKINS

HOUGHTON MIFFLIN COMPANY
BOSTON

For Page and Alec

Bibliography

Barrett, Norman. *Deserts, Picture Library*. New York: Franklin Watts, Inc., 1989.

Bonington, Chris. *Mountaineer*. San Francisco: Sierra Club Books, 1990.

Butterfield, Moira. *1000 Facts About the Earth*. New York: Scholastic, Inc., 1992.

Clifford, Nick. *Incredible Earth*. New York: DK Publishing, Inc., 1996.

Johnson, Jinny, ed. *What Makes the World Go Round?* New York: Henry Holt and Company, Inc., 1997.

Knapp, Brian. *Dune*. Danbury, Conn.: Grolier Educational Corporation, 1992.

Pringle, Laurence. *Rivers and Lakes*. Alexandria, Va.: Time-Life Books, Inc., 1985.

Simon, Seymour. *Mountains*. New York: William Morrow and Company, Inc., 1994.

Simon, Seymour. *Volcanoes*. New York: William Morrow and Company, Inc., 1988.

The text of this book is set in 16-point Palatino.
The illustrations are paper collage, reproduced in full color.

Library of Congress Cataloging-in-Publication Data
Jenkins, Steve, 1952 –
Hottest, coldest, highest, deepest / Steve Jenkins.
p. cm.
Summary: Describes some of the remarkable places on earth, including the hottest, coldest, windiest, snowiest, highest, and deepest.
RNF ISBN: 0-395-89999-0   PAP ISBN: 0-618-49488-X
Geography—Juvenile literature. [1. Geography—Miscellanea.]
I. Title.
G133.J46   1998
910 — dc21   97-53080   CIP AC

Manufactured in the United States of America
BVG 10 9 8 7

If you could visit any spot on earth, where would you go? What if you wanted to see some of the most amazing natural wonders in the world?

There are deserts that haven't seen rain for hundreds of years, and jungles where it pours almost every day. There are places so cold that even in the summer it's below freezing and spots where it's often hot enough to cook an egg on the ground. There are mountains many miles high and ocean trenches that are even deeper. You can find rivers thousands of miles long and waterfalls thousands of feet high.

Where are the very hottest and coldest, windiest and snowiest, highest and deepest places on earth? Travel the world and visit the planet's record holders.

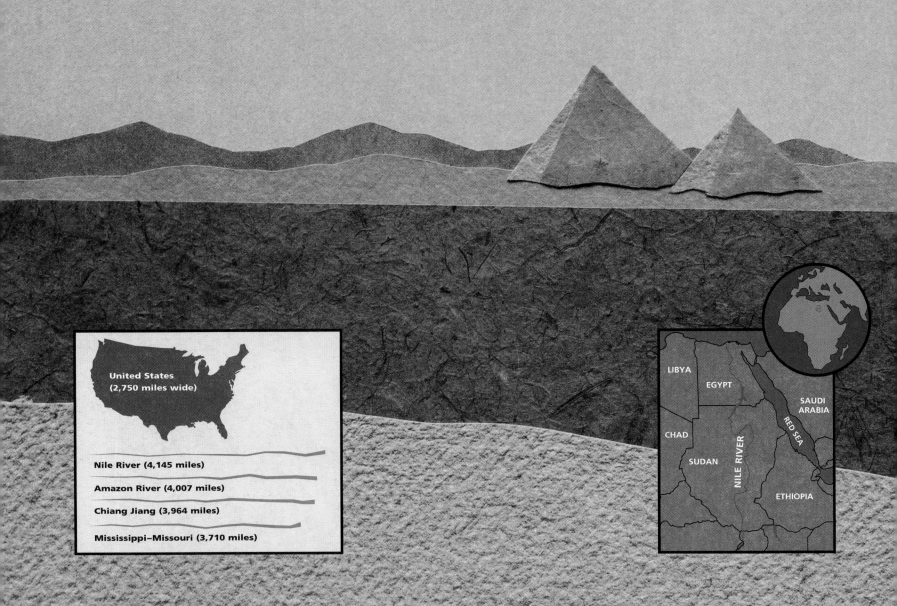

The Nile, in Africa, is the **longest** river in the world.
It is 4,145 miles long.

United States
(2,750 miles wide)

Nile River (4,145 miles)

Amazon River (4,007 miles)

Chiang Jiang (3,964 miles)

Mississippi–Missouri (3,710 miles)

LIBYA

EGYPT

SAUDI
ARABIA

CHAD

SUDAN

NILE RIVER

RED SEA

ETHIOPIA

The Amazon River, in South America, is not as long — 4,007 miles — but it is considered mightier because it carries half of all the river water in the world. The Chiang Jiang (Yangtze), in Asia (3,964 miles), and the Mississippi–Missouri, in the United States (3,710 miles), are the world's third and fourth longest rivers.

Lake Baikal, in Russia, is the world's **oldest** and **deepest** lake. The lake was formed about 25 million years ago. In one spot it is 5,134 feet deep.

The largest freshwater lake in the world is Lake Superior, one of the Great Lakes in North America (31,700 square miles), but Lake Baikal (5,500 square miles) contains more water than any other lake on earth — more than all five Great Lakes combined.

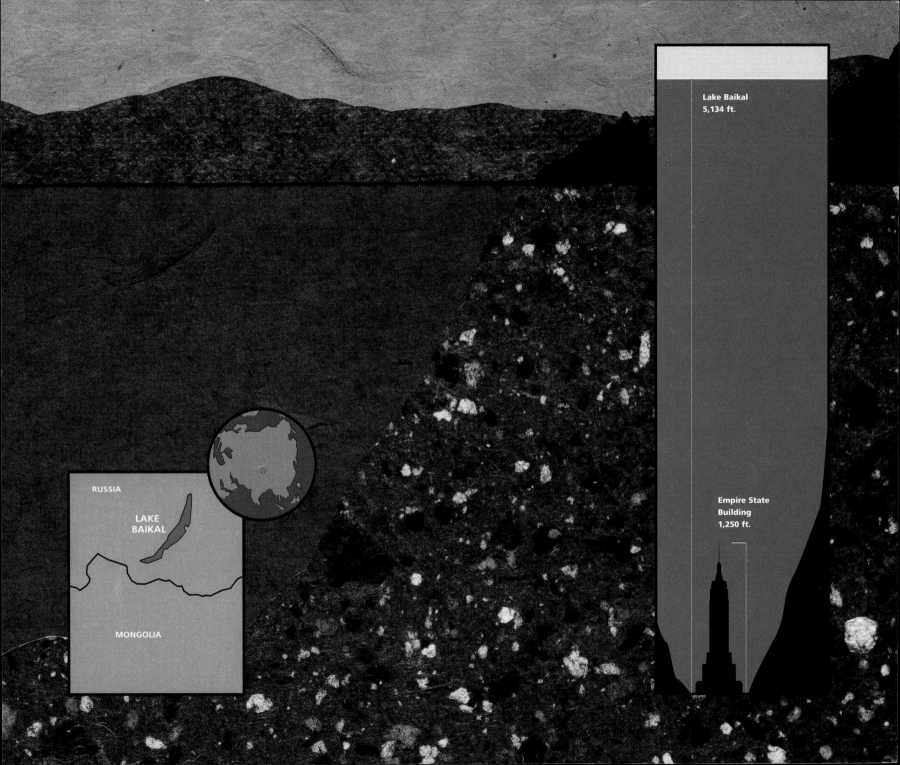

RUSSIA

LAKE
BAIKAL

MONGOLIA

Lake Baikal
5,134 ft.

Empire State
Building
1,250 ft.

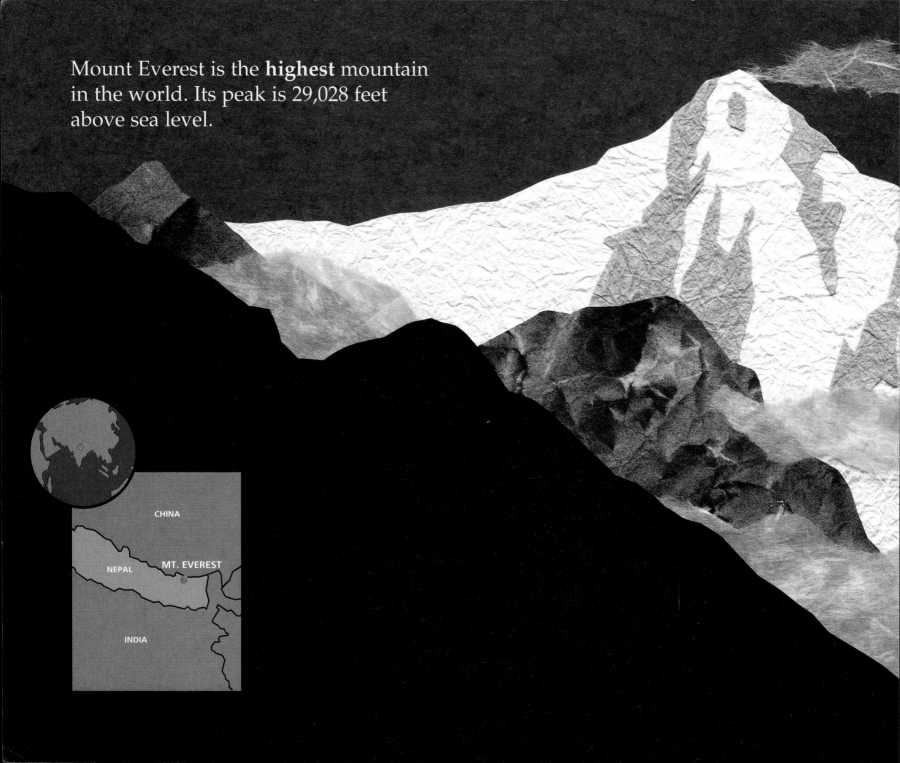

Mount Everest is the **highest** mountain in the world. Its peak is 29,028 feet above sea level.

CHINA

NEPAL   MT. EVEREST

INDIA

The highest mountain in North America is Mount McKinley (also called Denali), in Alaska, at 20,320 feet. Mount Whitney, in California, is the highest peak in the continental United States. Its summit is 14,491 feet above sea level.

Mt. Everest
29,028 ft.

Denali
20,320 ft.

Mt. Whitney
14,491 ft.

Empire
State
Building
1,250 ft.

Mauna Kea
33,476 ft. (from sea floor)

Mt. Everest
29,028 ft.

Sea Level

Denali
20,320 ft.

Sea Floor

Empire
State
Building
1,250 ft.

Mount Everest is considered the **highest** mountain — above sea level — in the world, but it's not really the **tallest**. Measured from its base on the floor of the ocean, Mauna Kea, in Hawaii, is 33,476 feet tall. Only the top 13,796 feet of Mauna Kea are above sea level.

Mount Everest rises from a plateau that is already 17,000 feet above sea level, so one would have to climb only about 12,000 feet to reach its summit. Mount McKinley, in Alaska, is almost 20,000 feet from base to summit.

KAUAI

OAHU

MOLOKAI

MAUI

MAUNA KEA

HAWAII

ALGERIA

AL AZIZIYAH

LIBYA

NIGER

CHAD

The **hottest** spot on the planet is Al Aziziyah, Libya, in the Sahara, where a temperature of over 136° F has been recorded.

The hottest temperature ever recorded in the United States is 134.6° F, in Death Valley, California.

136° F
134.6° F

98.6° F
Body temp.

68° F
Room temp.

32° F
Water freezes

The **coldest** place on the planet is Vostok, Antarctica. A temperature of 129° F below zero was recorded there.

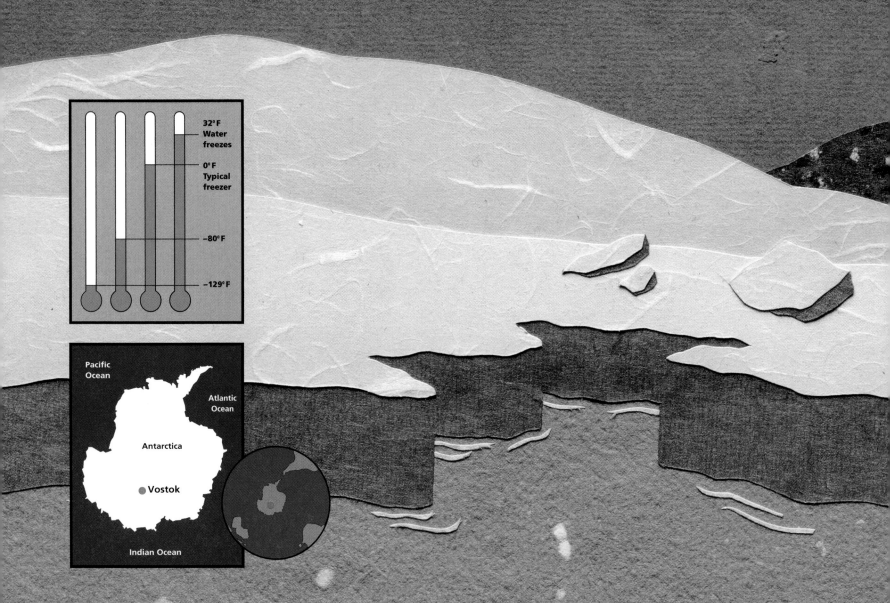

32° F
Water freezes

0° F
Typical freezer

−80° F

−129° F

Pacific Ocean

Atlantic Ocean

Antarctica

● Vostok

Indian Ocean

It is so cold at the South Pole that the average summer temperature is −58º F. The coldest temperature ever recorded in the United States is −80º F, at Prospect Creek Camp, Alaska.

The **wettest** place on earth is Tutunendo, Colombia, where an average of 463 inches of rain falls every year.

463 in.
Tutunendo
average annual
precipitation

36 in.
Chicago
average annual
precipitation

61 in.
La Réunion
one day rainfall

72 in.
Adult Man

Mount Wai-ale-ale, on the
island of Kauai in Hawaii,
has the most rainy days —
350 a year. On the island of
La Réunion, in the Indian
Ocean, more than 61 inches
of rain fell in a single day.

The **driest** place is the Atacama Desert, in Chile, where no rain has fallen for the last 400 years.

Any place that receives less than 10 inches of precipitation a year is considered a desert. The driest place in the United States is Death Valley, California, where only about 1½ inches of rain falls every year.

72 in.
Adult Man

10 in.
Desert precipitation

1½ in.
Death Valley average annual precipitation

PERU

BOLIVIA

ATACAMA

CHILE

ARGENTINA

10 mph
Breezy Day

150 mph
Severe Hurricane

231 mph
Mt. Washington

It is also very windy near the tops of the world's highest mountains, the Himalayas. Many of these peaks are tall enough to reach the jet stream, a narrow, strong air current that is found above 28,000 feet.

The **windiest** spot on earth is atop Mount Washington, in New Hampshire. A wind speed of 231 miles per hour has been recorded there.

CANADA

MAINE

MT. WASHINGTON

NEW YORK

ATLANTIC
OCEAN

The world's **highest** waterfall is Angel Falls, in Venezuela. It is 3,212 feet high.

Angel Falls
3,212 ft.

Victoria Falls
355 ft.

Niagara Falls
180 ft.

Empire State
Building
1,250 ft.

Angel Falls is more than seventeen times higher than Niagara Falls (180 feet), in New York State. Victoria Falls, in Zimbabwe, Africa, carries more water than any other waterfall. It is 355 feet high.

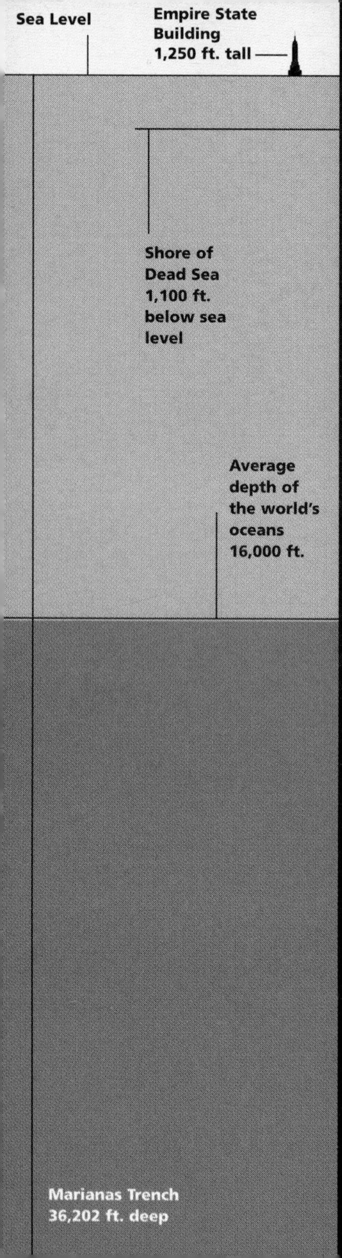

Sea Level

**Empire State
Building
1,250 ft. tall**

**Shore of
Dead Sea
1,100 ft.
below sea
level**

**Average
depth of
the world's
oceans
16,000 ft.**

**Marianas Trench
36,202 ft. deep**

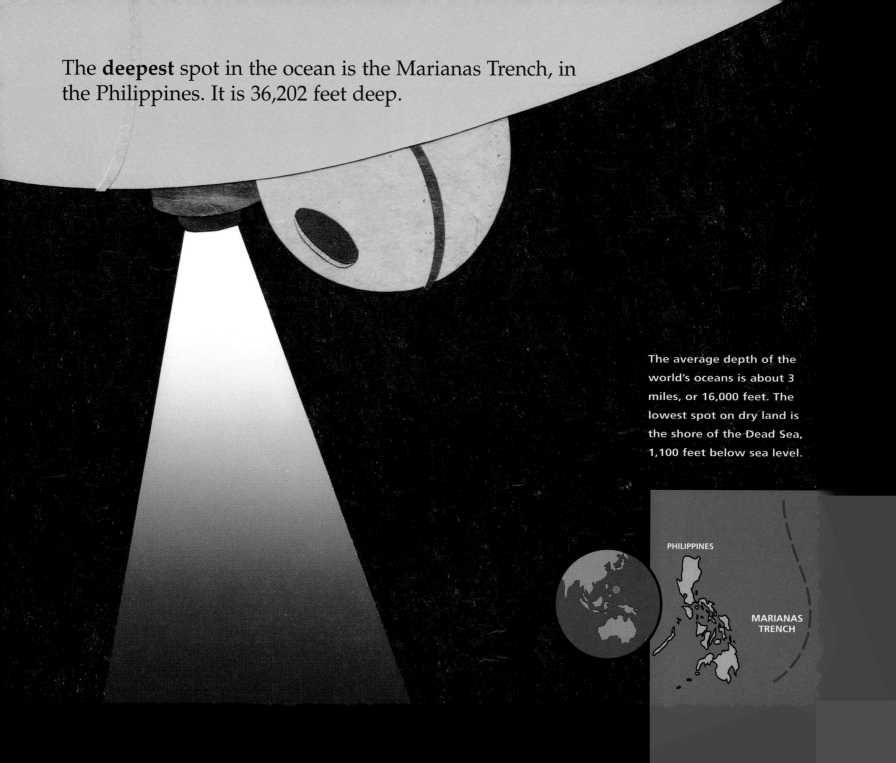

The **deepest** spot in the ocean is the Marianas Trench, in the Philippines. It is 36,202 feet deep.

The average depth of the world's oceans is about 3 miles, or 16,000 feet. The lowest spot on dry land is the shore of the Dead Sea, 1,100 feet below sea level.

PHILIPPINES

MARIANAS
TRENCH

The world's **most active** volcano is Sangay, in Ecuador. Since 1937 it has erupted once every 24 hours on average. It once erupted more than 400 times in a single day.

Other very active volcanoes include Colima, in Mexico (it has erupted regularly since 1560); Aso, in Japan (erupting since 533); and Mount Etna, in Italy (erupting regularly since 1500 B.C.).

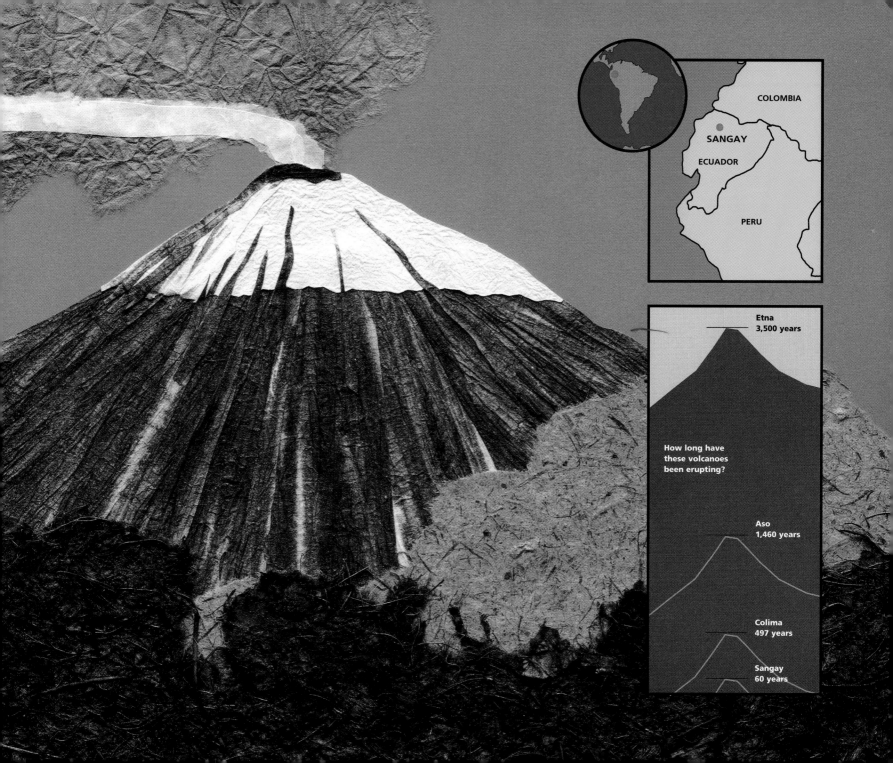

COLOMBIA

SANGAY

ECUADOR

PERU

Etna
3,500 years

How long have
these volcanoes
been erupting?

Aso
1,460 years

Colima
497 years

Sangay
60 years

The **most extreme tides** occur in the Bay of Fundy, in Nova Scotia, Canada. There the water level rises and falls more than 50 feet every 6 hours.

MAINE

NOVA SCOTIA

BAY
OF
FUNDY

The tide here comes in so fast that it can overtake a person trying to outrun it.

54 ft. tide
Bay of Fundy

3 ft.
Typical East Coast tide

6 ft.
Adult Man

CANADA

WASHINGTON

MT. RAINIER

OREGON

IDAHO

CALIFORNIA

100 ft.
Mt. Rainier
Record
1 year
snowfall

6 ft.
Adult Man

3 ft.
Typical
annual New
York City
snowfall

The **snowiest** place on earth is Mount Rainier, in Washington State. One year, more than 1,200 inches of snow fell there.

Mount Rainier is covered in snow the whole year. Some of the snow has formed glaciers, masses of ice that slowly move down the mountain under their own weight.

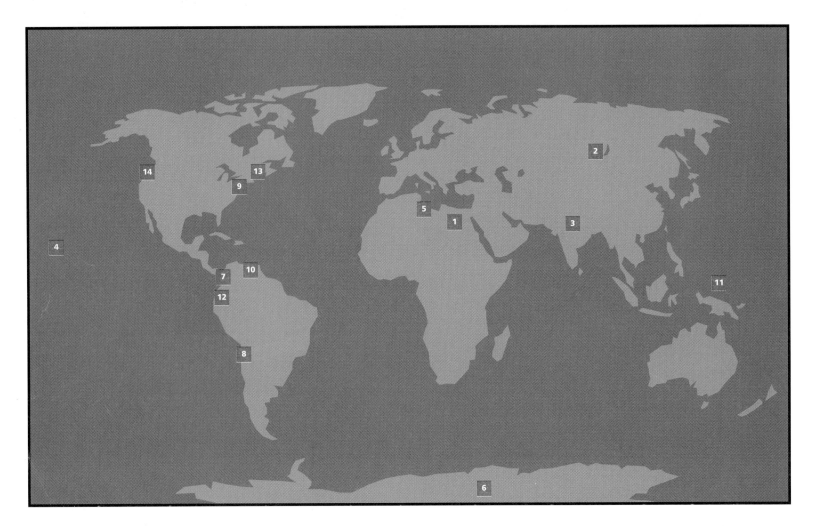

1 Nile River, Africa

2 Lake Baikal, Russia

3 Mount Everest, Nepal

4 Mauna Kea, Hawaii

5 Al Aziziyah, Libya

6 Vostok, Antarctica

7 Tutunendo, Colombia

8 Atacama Desert, Chile

9 Mount Washington, New Hampshire

10 Angel Falls, Venezuela

11 Marianas Trench, Philippines

12 Sangay, Ecuador

13 Bay of Fundy, Nova Scotia

14 Mount Rainier, Washington